Josh Swing

OPTIONS TRADING MADE EASY GUIDE FOR BEGINNERS

The complete and easy guide for beginners to building a passive income. Proven strategies to become a successful trader.

Table of Contents

INTRODUCTION 1
   Signs of Financial Slavery... 1
   Financial Freedom – What Is It and Why Do Only A Few People Have It 4
   Trading Options to Gain Financial Freedom 6
  CHAPTER 1: HOW TO INVEST AND MAKE PROFIT? 10
   What Are Options? 10
   Buying and Selling Options 11
  CHAPTER 2: HUGE MISTAKES THAT BEGINNERS USUALLY MAKE 13
   Putting All Your Eggs in One Basket 13
   Investing More than You Can 14
   Going All in Before You're Ready 14
   Failure to Study the Markets 15
   Not Getting Enough Time Value 15
   Not Having Adequate Liquidity 15
   Not Having a Grip on Volatility 16
   Failing to Have a Plan 16
   Ignoring Expiration Dates 16
   Overleveraging 17
   Buying Cheap Options 17
   Giving in to Panic 17
   Not Knowing How Much Cash You Can Afford to Lose 18
   Jumping into Puts Without Enough Experience and Cash to Cover Losses ... 18
   Piling It On 19
   Staying in a Written Contract When You Should Get Out 19
  CHAPTER 3: HOW TO GET STARTED WITH OPTION TRADING 20
   Look for An Options Trading Broker. 20
   Do Some Testing on The Brokerage Platform? 22
   Be Approved to Trade Options. 22
   Get A Clear Understanding of The Technical Analysis. 23
   Take Advantage of Simulated Trading Accounts. 23
   Utilize Limit Orders. 23
   Revise Your Strategies with Time. 24
   Register and Join in Options Trading Platforms. 24
   Study and Learn About Trading Metrics. 24
  CHAPTER 4: VARIOUS TYPES OF OPTION CONTRACTS 26
    ▪ *Call Options:* 26
    ▪ *Put Options:* 27
    ▪ *Over the Counter Options:* 27

- *Exchange-Traded Options:* *28*
- *Cash Settled Options:* *28*
- *Employee Stock Options:* *28*
- *European Style Options:* *29*
- *American Style Options:* *29*
- *Expiry-Based Options:* *30*
- *Exotic Options:* *30*
- *Underlying Protection Options:* *31*

CHAPTER 5: OPTIONS TRADING JARGON 33

Terms and expressions *33*

Ask 33

Assignment 34

At the Money 34

Bid Price 34

Break Even Point 34

Call 34

Commission 35

Delta 35

Early Exercise 35

Exercise 35

Expiration Date 35

JUN 70 35

In the Money (Call) 36

In the Money (Put) 36

Index Options 36

Intrinsic Value 36

LEAP 36

Legs 37

Long 37

Margin Requirement 37

Option Chain 37

Out-of-the-Money 37

Premium 38

Put 38

Roll a Long Position 38

Roll a Short Position 38

Series 39

Short 39

Strike Price 39

00040000 39

00005600 39

Time Value 39

Time Decay 40

Underlying 40

Weekly 40

CHAPTER 6: TRADING STRATEGIES 41
Married Put 42
Bull Call Spread 43
Bear Put Spread 43
Protective Collar 44
Straddle 45
Strangle 45
Butterfly Spread 46
Iron Condor 47
Iron Butterfly 47
ROI or Return on Investment 47

CHAPTER 7: AT THE MONEY, OUT OF THE MONEY, IN THE MONEY 49
In the Money 49
Out of the Money 51
At the Money 52
Time Value 52

CHAPTER 8: VOLATILITY IN THE MARKETS 54
What is Volatility in the Markets? 54
How Option Volatility Determines Which Option Strategy to Use ... 59
*How Option Volatility Can Alert You in Advance to Significant Market Moves
.... 61*

CHAPTER 9: OPTIONS PRICING 63
Market Price of Shares 63
Implied Volatility 67
Time Decay 70
Risk-Free Rate 71

CHAPTER 10: ADVANCED TRADING STRATEGIES 72
Combining Fundamental and Technical Analysis for Advanced Trading 73
How Fundamental and Technical Analysis Complements Each Other 74

- Analytical Trading Example 75
- The Bottom Line 78
- Advanced Trading Indicators 79
- CHAPTER 11: STRIKE PRICE 81
  - What is Strike Price? 81
- CHAPTER 12: OPTION TRADER MINDSET 85
  - The Traits of a Successful Options Trader 86
  - Dream Big 89
- CHAPTER 13: BUYING AND SELLING PUTS 92
  - Buying Puts 92
  - Selling Puts 94
- CHAPTER 14: PASSIVE INCOME 95
  - Steps in How You Can Train the Passive Income 99
- CHAPTER 15: WHY OPTIONS TRADING IS THE WORLD'S GREATEST MONEY-MAKING MACHINE? 102
  - Options Provide Leverage 102
  - Options are Inexpensive 103
  - Options Prices Change in Big Ways 103
  - Options Have a Higher ROI 104
  - Options are Flexible 105
  - Options are Fast 106

CONCLUSION 107

Introduction

Financial freedom. Many seek it but few have it. That is because the secrets behind obtaining it are closely guarded by those who have it. This book is about exposing one true and reliable way that you can earn the financial security and independence you need to take control of the way you live your daily life.

Signs of Financial Slavery

The first active step needed to get started on a journey to financial freedom is acknowledging that you are not financially stable or free. This is a hard pill for some people to swallow and so they avoid acknowledging it even with the overwhelming evidence to support the state.

Facing this fact is not about demeaning your integrity or bring you down. It is about giving you a foundation to start with so that you can build the financial security you need. This knowledge is needed to show you where you currently stand financially and what your resources are so that you can develop a plan to get where you need and want to be.

The following conditions are those that chain many people to financial slavery:

- Living paycheck to paycheck. People who live this way do not have an emergency fund and typically have accompanying credit card debt because they need to subsidize their expenses, which are higher than their income. Many people live this way. More than 40% of American households could not cover a $400 expense such as medical bills or car repairs if it came up unexpectedly in 2017.

- Not having enough saved up to sustain their lifestyle if they were to lose their job. People such as these do not have enough money accumulated to take time away from working daily. This is the reason why most people are in careers and jobs that bring them no joy. They need the salary to keep a roof over their heads and food in their belly and so, they deal with the circumstances that make them unhappy.

- Not being able to pursue the activities and adventures that bring happiness while still saving and accumulating wealth. These types of people are stuck in a cycle of trading their daily hours for money while still being unable to enjoy the money that they earn because it is not enough to allow them this enjoyment and still pay the bills.

- Having inflexible schedules. Most people are stuck in a cycle of working every day and going home to come back to work the next day. They have to give this time to earn an income and therefore, become chained to their jobs.

- Not being able to retire comfortably at the desired age. The world over, the average age for retirement is 65 years old. However, many people are not expected to live even 20 years passed that age. That does not live much time to enjoy a life free of accumulating wealth. The sadder fact is that most people do not retire with enough money saved up to enjoy the things that they want after retirement. Some others still have to work a job even after this age to sustain themselves. Financially free people can retire at the age that they want rather than one that is dictated by someone else. They also have the capital available to do the things they want to do and still have income coming to them on a more passive basis.

- Spending more money than earned. This results because people want to live the lifestyle that they want but cannot afford or people needing to subsidize their income to cater to their needs. To build wealth, you cannot have more money going out than coming in. Signs that your spending exceeds your income include having a budget based on your salary, having an expense list that exceeds your net income, carrying a balance on your credit card, having rent or mortgage that is more than 30% of your net income and buying things to impress or keep up with other people.

Are you a slave to your finances? Would you like to use your time in other ways while still earning a steady and growing income? Can you use an extra income to develop the lifestyle you want?

Answering yes to any of these income questions or relating to even just one of the conditions stated above means you can use the advice and strategies outlined in this book.

Financial Freedom – What Is It and Why Do Only A Few People Have It

Having financial freedom is more than just having a 6-month emergency fund saved up and your debt cleared. Financial freedom means taking control of your time and finances so that you can do the things that you want to do rather than what your bank account figure dictates. Being financially free means you do not need to trade your time for money.

To be able to gain this financial freedom, you need to have financial security. Financial security is the condition whereby you support the standard of living you want now and in the future by having stable sources of income and other resources available to you. That means not living paycheck to paycheck. It means not having to worry about where your next dollar will come from. It means having a huge weight lifted off your shoulders because you know there are resources that you can leverage to get the things that you want and need.

People who have financial freedom are also financially independent. Financial independence is the state of having personal wealth to maintain the lifestyle and the standard of living you want without actually having to trade your daily hours for money. The assets and resources that you have generated will gain that income for you so that your income remains far greater than your expenses. In essence, being financially independent means that you can go for a prolonged time without trading time for money and still have the standard of living that you want. That you can go on a year-long vacation and still be secure in the knowledge that your wealth is still growing.

To be financially independent, you have to have:

- An emergency fund that can sustain your lifestyle for an extended period (years).
- Assets that produce income for you on a daily, weekly, monthly, and yearly basis.
- Very little or zero debt.

Very few people on the planet are financially secure and independent. More than 1 billion people live in extreme poverty. In 2015, it was estimated that more than 10% of the global population lived on less than US$1.90 per day.

Despite these statistics, there is hope. This hope comes from the fact that this statistic goes down every year. In fact, in 2019 less than 8% of the global population lived in extreme poverty. This is largely attributed to the fact that people being more educated about their options and are not just accepting of these poor circumstances.

Despite this improvement, most of the global population still trades their time for an hourly wage. The income earned from this is not sustainable nor will it allow them to live the standard of life that they would like. They will not be able to retire comfortably. There is no power or security in living this way.

Financially free people have learned and harnessed the power of passive income. Passive income is wealth that is generated from little to no effort or earned in the way of exchanging time for money over the long term. While it might take a massive amount of time and effort to establish in the beginning, passive income allows you to earn money even while you sleep with little to no daily effort required for its maintenance.

The beauty of passive income is that it is not only limited to one income bracket or portion of the population. Anyone can develop passive income as long as they develop the right mindset and is willing to put in the time and effort to learn and be consistent in pursuing this standard of living.

Trading Options to Gain Financial Freedom

Trading options has the great potential to be a form of passive income. This is the complete opposite to active income, which is what most people engage in. Active income is one where a person invests time in exchange for money. We have deliberated the pitfalls of this and seen why it should not be a person's only form of income.

Passive income allows you to still enjoy your time as you dictate while earning money. It comes to you on automatic even while you sleep. While it usually takes time, effort, and maybe monetary input at the beginning, over the long-term, if done right, you can sustain the lifestyle you want if you put forth that investment now.

Passive income:

- Gives you the platform to gain financial stability, security, and independence.
- Gives you the freedom to do whatever you wish with your time without the worry of sustaining your financial life.

- Gives you the freedom to pursue the career, hobbies, and other activities you love and enjoy rather than having to trade your time for money.
- Allows you to secure your financial future, thus getting rid of your worry, stress, and anxiety in that department.
- Gives you the flexibility to live and work from anywhere in the world, typically. The bonus of this means you get to travel if that is a pursuit you would like to take on while still earning.

Trading options can give you the benefits listed above and thus, light the way to your financial freedom.

As I mentioned above, having a growth mindset means that you openly receive information from other people to better yourself and your financial life. I am sharing my knowledge with you in this insightful guide because I have implemented these same strategies with tremendous success. It is not a perfect system, but it is one that works well if done right and consistently.

Before I invite you to delve in, let me say this... To gain the most benefit from reading the information to come, you need to cultivate the growth mindset mentioned above. You have to also treat this like a business, not a side gig. This is not a hobby nor something that you are just dabbling in. Make the effort and time you invest count. Make it consistent and be persistent. Set a schedule and work on this every day. Make goals for yourself and give yourself a timeline for your accomplishments. Stay focused and committed.

The world's wealth is majorly divided into a small part of the population.

Only that small percentage has financial freedom. You can put yourself and your family in that small percentile using this method for passive income. I have faith that you can do it as long as you put in that initial effort. The question is – do you believe that you can do too? Can you envision yourself as the person who has attained financial freedom in the future and is living the life you want?

Answer *YES* to both these questions and believe in that answer, I implore you!

Now, without further ado, let's jump into this invaluable guide so that you can start the future you desire today.

Chapter 1: How to Invest and Make Profit?

What Are Options?

An option is a contract that provides the purchaser the right, but not the responsibility, to sell or buy an asset subject to a precise price no later than a specified date. An option, such as stock or bond, is a type of security. It is also a contract that comes with strictly defined terms and properties.

After all, a contract for stock options can take two forms: call options and orders. In both cases, you've got the right, but not the obligation, to buy or sell the shares subject to a predetermined price. The default price is also called a strike price.

An essential feature of options, whatever their type, is the expiration date, a date when the option expires and is no longer valuable. Before the expiration date, investors give another person the option during the month to make a profit. However, due to decreased time and other reasons, the option will lose value while the expiration date is set.

For example, let's say on June 1, 2020, ABC traded at $ 10 per share. You can buy a call option on this stock exchange that allows you to buy 100 shares at any time (for example, August 23, 2020) for $ 12 per share. Why would you want to do this? Well, you might think that the ABC Company is underestimated and correct. Then buy at your option and wait. If 45 days later, ABC Company now trades at $ 15 a share, then you can exercise your stock purchase option to $ 12 and you have made a significant profit. However, if ABC Company is trading below $ 12, it will not exercise your option and will be useless.

In options terminology, the first is the price of the option contract. It changes continuously depending on market conditions and what the underlying security is doing. The first is equal to the intrinsic value (the amount of the option is in cash) + the time value (the more extended time remains until the expiration date, the higher). When you sell your option, you must subtract the amount of premium from the profit.

Buying and Selling Options

In options trading, you can be the buyer or seller of the option.

If you purchase a call option, you acquire the right to purchase the underlying shares (or any other underlying instruments) at the strike price specified not later than the expiration date of the option. If you purchase a put option, you have the right to sell the shares at the strike price no later than the expiration date. However, you can also sell the option to another buyer or drop it.

Another scenario is when selling or writing options. In these cases, you are required to abide by the terms of the option contract if the buyer wishes to apply it. Thus, if you sell a call option, you have to sell the underlying assets at the strike cost to the buyer. And in the position of a put option, you have to buy the stock at the strike price. If you write options, you must understand that it is up to the buyer to decide whether to exercise the contract or not and he must be ready to abide by the terms of the contract. Nevertheless, it is possible to buy another contract to offset your obligation and, in this way, you can get out of the deal.

Chapter 2: Huge Mistakes that Beginners Usually Make

Trading options are more involved than trading stocks, so there are ample opportunities to make mistakes. It's important to take the approach of going small and slow at first so that you don't lose the shirt off your back. That said, if you run into mistakes, don't get too down about it. Dust yourself off and get up to fight another day. With that said, let's have a look at some common mistakes and how to avoid them.

Putting All Your Eggs in One Basket

While there is a difference between investing and trading, traders can learn a few things from our investor brothers (and most people are a little of both anyway). Don't let everything ride on one trade. If you take all the money you have and invest it in buying options for one stock, you're making a big mistake. Doing that is very risky, and as a beginning trader, you're going to want to mitigate your risk as much as possible. Betting on one stock may pay off sometimes, but more times than not it's going to lead you into bankruptcy territory.

Investing More than You Can

It's easy to get excited about options trading. The chances to make fast money and the requirements that you analyze the markets can be very enticing. Oftentimes that leads people into getting more excited than they should. A good rule to follow with investing is to make sure that you're setting aside enough money to cover living expenses every month, with a security fund for emergencies. Don't bet the farm on some sure thing by convincing yourself that you'll be able to make back twice as much money and so cover your expenses. Things don't always work out.

Going All in Before You're Ready

Another mistake is failing to take the time to learn options trading in real-time. Just like getting overly excited can cause people to bet too much money or put all their money on one stock, some people are impatient and don't want to take the time to learn the options markets by selling covered calls. It's best to start with covered calls and then move slowly to small deals buying call options. Leave put options until you've gained some experience.

Failure to Study the Markets

Remember, you need to be truly educated to make good options trades. That means you'll need to know a lot about the companies that you're either trying to profit from or that you're shorting. Options trading isn't possible without some level of guesswork, but make your guesses, educated guesses, and don't rely too much on hunches.

Not Getting Enough Time Value

Oftentimes, whether you're trading puts or calls, the time value is important. A stock may need an adequate window of time to beat the stock price, whether it's going above it or plunging below it. When you're starting and don't know the markets as well as a seasoned trader, you should stick to options you can buy that have a longer time before expiring.

Not Having Adequate Liquidity

Sometimes beginning investors overestimate their ability to play the options markets. Remember that if you buy an option, to make it work for you—you're going to need money on hand to buy stocks when the iron is hot. And you're going to need to buy 100 shares for every option contract. Before entering into the contract, make sure that you're going to be able to exercise your option.

Not Having a Grip on Volatility

If you don't understand volatility and its relation to premium pricing, you may end up making bad trades.

Failing to Have a Plan

Trading seems exciting, and when you're trading, you may lose the investors' mentality. However, traders need to have a strategic plan as much as investors do. Before trading, make sure that you have everything in place, including knowing what your goals are for the trades, having pre-planned exit strategies, developing criteria for getting into a trade so that you're not doing it on a whim or based on emotion.

Ignoring Expiration Dates

It sounds crazy, but many beginners don't keep track of the expiration date. Would you hate to see a stock go up in price, and then hope it keeps going up, and it does, only to find out that your expiration date passed before you exercised your option?

Overleveraging

It's easy to spend huge amounts of money in small increments. This is true when it comes to trading options. Since stocks are more expensive, it's possible to get seduced by purchasing low priced options. After all, options are available at a fraction of the cost that is required to buy stocks. And you might keep on purchasing them until you're overleveraged.

Buying Cheap Options

In many cases, buying cheap things isn't a good strategy. If you're buying a used car, while you might occasionally find a great car that is a good buy, in most cases, a car is cheap for a reason. The same applies to options trading. When it comes to options, a cheap premium probably denotes the option is out of the money. Sure, you save some money on a cheap premium, but when the expiration date comes, you might see the real reason the option contract was a cheap buy. Of course, as we described earlier, there may be cases where cheaper options can rebound and become profitable by the time the expiry date arrives. But taking chances like that is best left to experienced traders.

Giving in to Panic

Remember that you have the right to buy or sell a stock if you've purchased an option. Some beginners panic and exercise their right far too early. This can happen because of fears that they'll be missing out on an opportunity with a call option, or because of fears that a stock won't keep going down on a put.

Not Knowing How Much Cash You Can Afford to Lose

Going into options trading blindly is not a smart move. With each option trade you make, you need to have a clear idea of how much cash you have on hand to cover losses and exercising your options. You'll also want to know how much cash you can afford to lose if things go south.

Jumping into Puts Without Enough Experience and Cash to Cover Losses

Remember, if you're selling puts, you will have to buy the stock at the strike price if the buyer exercises their option. This is a huge risk. The stock could have plunged in value, and you're going to have to buy the stock at the strike price, possibly leaving you with huge losses. Don't go into selling puts with your eyes closed beginners are better off avoiding selling puts. But if you must do it, make sure you can absorb the losses when you bet wrong.

Piling It On

Most beginner mistakes are related to panic. If you're looking at losses on options, some beginners double and triple up, hoping to make it up when things turn better. Instead, they end up losing more money. Instead of giving in to panic, learn when to cut your losses and re-evaluate your trading strategy.

Staying in a Written Contract When You Should Get Out

If you've sold an option and it's looking like you might face a loss, you can always get out of it by selling.

Chapter 3: How to Get Started with Option Trading

Now with the necessary knowledge on options trading. There are a few details on how to start an options trading journey.

Look for An Options Trading Broker.

The key to successful options trading is your broker. There exist legit and non-legit brokers in options trading. The following are some tips for selecting a good broker:

Do some research on the broker first. Be keen and alert before opening a brokerage options trading platform. Different brokers will approach you with different platforms. Do not rush or assume everything is functional; do some research on the best brokers. Make sure you spend your cash well by paying for a good options trading platform. It will help you a lot because your trading performance depends on your platform. Choose a broker with good ratings.

Charges lower commissions. Some brokers tend to exploit traders by charging high commissions to beginners. Weigh different commission offers of various brokers before settling on one. Some even charge no commission to traders. Prefer brokers with fewer commissions. Payment of high commissions periodically can mess you up with losses, and you may find it even hard to secure your trading capital. Do not accept to pay high commissions. You also need to do some savings other than wasting money while paying commissions.

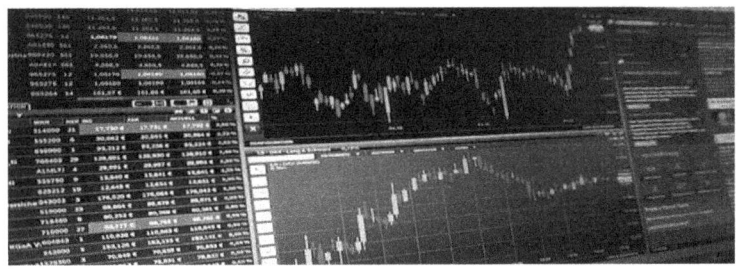

A simple user interface platform. There is a wide variety of software with different functionalities and features. Some software has a simple user interface, while others are too complex for you to use. Choose a platform with a simple and clear user interface that enables you to make your trades with less struggle. Some platforms can waste your precious time when you struggle too much searching on the Internet on how you operate them. Make your work easier by handling software that is according to your level. Trading tools for research. Consider factors like tools that are present on the platform. Do not purchase a platform with no tools. It will be hard for you. Platform tools ease your trading and make your performance excellent. The tools here may include charting tools, research tools, and even tools that alert you on any market changes that may arise.

Do Some Testing on The Brokerage Platform?

Do not be that kind of a careless trader who does things for the sake of doing with no precautions. You need to be cautious enough since this is an income-generating activity. You should test on a brokerage software before making up your mind about purchasing it. Check on the software's reliability and stability and be 100% sure that this is the platform you will use for your trading. Ensure the software is not that type of platform that crashes down unexpectedly. You might miss crucial trade while fixing your software.

Be Approved to Trade Options.

You need to be approved by the broker in charge before purchasing and offering options for sale. They usually have ways of passing you, like checking your experience and the money you have. It aids in avoiding risks for the customers. You cannot escape this step.

Get A Clear Understanding of The Technical Analysis.

Options trading is a specialized field. You need to have the special analysis techniques of trading options. The technical aspects include reading charts, know about the volume of stock, and also moving averages. Trading charts mostly analyze price behavior in the market. You will handle the aspects many times while trading. Perfect your technical knowledge and be cautious with them.

Take Advantage of Simulated Trading Accounts.

Using real accounts when starting options trading is a risky game. You can lose a lot of cash within a short time duration. Simulated accounts exist for a reason. You should test your trading skills in the mock accounts, learn a few tricks, and perfect your skills. The advantage of using a simulated account is that there is no loss of money since it mostly provides virtual money. When everything works out well, face real trading and shine.

Utilize Limit Orders.

It is risky to rely on market prices since price behavior change with time.

A limit order enables you to purchase market securities at an agreed price. Using this type of order shuns you from incurring losses in options trading.

Revise Your Strategies with Time.

After entering into the options trading, with time, you need to revise your strategy. Utilize the working strategy more often and get rid of unsuccessful trading strategies. You should not have many plans that do not bring excellent performance. Few working strategies are better than having multiple ones that do not help you.

Register and Join in Options Trading Platforms.

Joining forums comprised of other options traders is another way of how to get started in options trading. Forums are platforms for different people with different experiences and opinions. You can learn mistakes made by others in trading. It is part of growing in options trading.

Study and Learn About Trading Metrics.

Having your returns maximized is also another way of getting started in options trading. Traders frequently use different trading metrics, such as delta, gamma, theta, and Vega. You should learn and practice them for massive returns.

Chapter 4: Various Types of Option Contracts

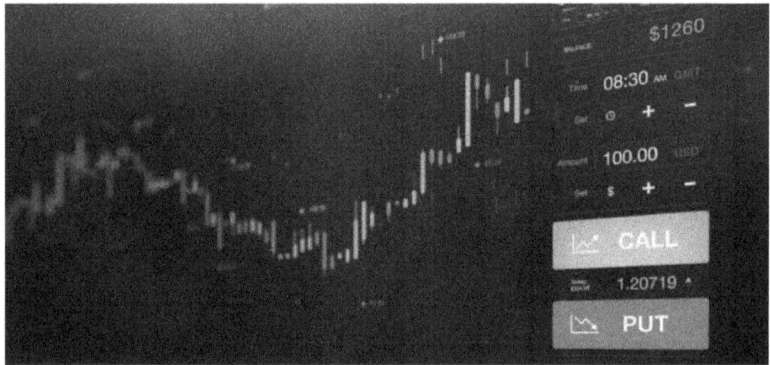

The classification system of options takes a step further than just utilizing the approach used in identifying them for trading. The underlying functionality they relate to and the expiration period they have are the additional tools used to distinguish the different options. This expands individual findings to several kinds of options that exist around the universe. For a person to understand the basics of options trading, these options can be put forth. They consist of:

- **Call Options:**

Call Options are defined by making available the right to buy the negotiated asset on a date in the future to an individual. The acquired commodities appear to have a value that is already settled upon. Some situations can make a person make a call on investment. The most common scenario is when one anticipates that the asset can increase its value after a certain period. A distinctive and rare feature of calls is that they've had have an expiry date that depends on the contract an individual has entered into. It is also possible to buy the asset being pursued before the expiration date.

- **Put Options:**

Puts are usually the exact opposite of calls. The right to sell the underlying assets is granted to the individual who owns the put option. The sale method tends to have a negotiated price for the potential actions that have been allocated. Throughout the financial markets, this situation appears during fascinating periods. When one has speculated on the value of assets to fall, a person is likely to fall under set action. There are parallels between calls and puts, despite being the reverse of the call. A significant joint event is that the time set is constrained to each of them. Therefore, on the agreement one has entered into, puts have an expiry date.

- **Over the Counter Options:**

Mostly in the over-the-counter markets, this type of exchange option is traded. These are usually standard features, which are exacerbated by counter-trade options, make them rare to the public as a whole.

Compared with other options, the provisions of contracts in these types of options appear to be more complicated.

▪ Exchange-Traded Options:

These are also well recognized to many financial market participants as listed options around the globe. It is termed as one of the most commonly used types of options known to individuals. There are many options contracts on public trading exchanges that have been listed. Those are the types of options described as options for currency trading. With the help of subtle traders, they can be bought or sold by anyone.

▪ Cash Settled Options:

The actual transfer of the assets being exchanged does not differentiate these types of contracts from each other. It is possible to link what happens in a cash-settled option to the name it has. In this type of option, revenue created by the effective party is obtained in cash forms. This type of options trading is affected by certain factors. When the asset being passed is expensive or difficult to move to the other party, it is about the situation.

▪ Employee Stock Options:

It is known that these kinds of stock options are presented to employees.

This contract will be awarded by the organization they work for as an agent of a specific company that provides the option. Its general use is to facilitate the remuneration of the staff. It goes ahead as incentives or advantages are offered to employees of a specific company. It has many advantages because it attracts people to work for organizations providing such services.

- **European Style Options:**

The same flexibility that peoples who use American-style contracts have is not granted to people who are offered these options. For this type of option, the timeline is rigorous. Any person who uses contracts of the European type shall exchange their underlying assets only on the date of expiry and not before or after that date.

- **American Style Options:**

The American style has nothing to do with buying and selling agreements as it deepens down to options. It targets its lenses according to the terms stated in the contractual terms of the agreement. Necessary information at this point is that options in their contracts come with an expiry date, allowing a trader the right to buy or sell an underlying asset on the stock markets. After the contract's expiry date in the American style alternative, every person has the right to exercise his or her contract. A retailer using American style options seems to be supported by the listed flexibility.

▪ Expiry-Based Options:

As per their expiry dates, it is possible to classify contracts. This applies to such irregularities that a trader is presumed to exchange under an arrangement concerning the agreed duration. The contacts decided that the trade opportunities appeared to be different from the periods they had. They compose:

- Daily options are based on the cycles organized in the exchange contracts and specified. In a financial year, one will likely have four months of expiry from which to choose.
- Weekly Options were implemented in 2005 and often referred to as Weeklies. As conventional alternatives, they have the exact qualities, in which they are believed to have all timing. Weeklies appear to be used with financial instrument limitations.
- Quarterly options: listed on financial markets with expiry dates close to or near the fiscal quarters. Some people call them every week, and on the last day of expiration, they terminate.

▪ Exotic Options:

This is a term that describes contract options that have been personally customized by options traders. The effect of this tailoring makes the contracts very complicated. In some instances, they are called Non-

Standardized Options. Additional unusual arrangements are available which are only present in the OTC (Over The Counter) markets. That said, some of these options contracts have started to be popular in the current financial markets. These possibilities include:

- Binary options: the owner of the underlying financial assets shall, if the contract expires, pay a fixed sum of money.
- Barrier Options: payment is sometimes granted to the holder of this contract form before the contract's price is exceeded.
- Compound Options: the type of trading option in which another option is the underlying financial asset.
- Choose Options: This method of trading of options enables a financial trader to decide at any time whether to call or put in.

▪ Underlying Protection Options:

A stock option is a general one that becomes the focus as people start to think about trading options. That is where the associated underlying assets can, as a financial instrument, be publicly listed. This is a fundamental awareness of individuals who have invested in this medium of commerce. In this case, there are several types of options involved, including:

- A publicly-traded company owns stock options; the shares; the underlying assets exchanged under this agreement are generated.

- Basket option: this is a sort of trading strategy with many financial instruments being the underlying assets.
- Currency options: these contracts are radically different from other options. That is because a trader is given the freedom to sell or purchase currency. On negotiated contract terms, trade is made.
- Index options, which tend to be somewhat equivalent to stock options. There is one distinction, however that depicts the blurred line. Since stocks are not the corresponding form of security being exchanged, separation occurs; instead, separation occurs. For a business, they are the indicators.
- Commodity Option: The assets highlighted in this form of options trading appear to be physical commodities.
- Future options: The underlying asset used in this type of trading option is the futures contract. A future choice also has the potential to allow an investor to benefit from a future agreement.

Chapter 5: Options Trading Jargon

Every industry has its specialized lingo, and options trading is no exception. Let's give a quick overview that will help you understand what is being deliberated when reading about options and help you navigate the markets effectively.

Terms and expressions

Ask

The price that a seller is asking for security or put another way the smallest price a seller is willing to accept to sell it.

Assignment

When the buyer of an options contract exercises their option, a notice is sent to the seller. The seller is then obligated to dispose of (in the case of a call) or purchase (in the case of a put) stocks at the strike price.

At the Money

This means that the current market price is equal to the strike price.

Bid Price

This term refers to the optimum amount that a dealer is willing to shell out for security.

Break Even Point

When neither a profit nor loss has been realized.

Call

The buyer of a call option has the right to buy 100 shares of a stock at the strike price at any time before the options contract expires. This is an option, so the buyer does not have to buy the shares. The seller of a call contract must buy the shares under any circumstances up to the expiration of the contract if the buyer exercises their right before the contract expires.

Commission

A fee that is charged by a brokerage firm to execute an option order on an exchange.

Delta

If the underlying stock changes by a point in value, the delta is the change in the value of the option.

Early Exercise

If an options contract is exercised before the expiration date, it is said to be early.

Exercise

The buyer of the option exercises their right to buy stock for a call or sell the stock for a put.

Expiration Date

Options contracts expire on the third Friday of every month. When you see an option quote such as:

JUN 70

That means that the option expires on the third Friday in June, with a strike price of $70.

In the Money (Call)

This refers to the occurrence of when the current market price exceeds the strike price. This is the gross profit per share (not including premium and other fees).

In the Money (Put)

For a put contract, it is in-the-money when the current stock price is less than the strike price.

Index Options

An index option doesn't have individual stocks as the underlying. Instead, the underlying is an index like the NASDAQ. An index option can't be exercised until the expiry date.

Intrinsic Value

An apt example would be – if the current price is at $10, then the market price is at $20, the intrinsic value would be $10. If the current price were $25, the intrinsic value would be $15.

LEAP

A LEAP is a long-term equity anticipation security. These are long term options contracts. LEAP contracts can last as long as three years. LEAPS are generally more expensive than most options, because of the longtime value which gives them more time to be "in the money."

Legs

A leg is one part of a position when there are two or more options or positions in the underlying stock.

Long

Long means ownership when it is held in your account. You can belong on a stock or an option.

Margin Requirement

If you are selling options, you will be required to deposit some cash with the brokerage to cover your positions. In other words, it is cash in your account with the brokerage to buy or sell shares as required by your obligations in the options contract.

Option Chain

An option chain is something you'll look at when viewing available options online. It's a table for the options available for a given underlying stock. Given the expiration date, the option chain will include all puts and calls, and available strike prices.

Out-of-the-Money

This is the amount that a stock price is below the strike price for a call, or above the strike price for a put. If your price $50 but the market is

$40, you're "out of the money" $10. If your strike price for a put is $50, but the market price is $60, you're out of the money $10.

Premium

This is the price paid per share for an options contract. Since the contract has 100 shares, the price paid, or the total premium is 100 times the premium. The seller can keep the premium regardless of whether or not the buyer exercises their options.

Put

The buyer of a put option has the privilege to sell 100 shares at the strike price on or before the expiry date. The seller of a put option has to buy 100 shares if required by the buyer.

Roll a Long Position

Rolling a long position means to sell options and then acquire others with the same underlying stock but with different strike prices and expiration dates.

Roll a Short Position

Rolling a short position means buying to close an existing position and selling to open new positions with different strike prices and expiration dates "rolled out" in time.

Series

Options are grouped in series on the markets. Options in the same series can be calls or puts, but they have the same expiration date and strike price.

Short

Selling a security that you don't own.

Strike Price

It is the amount per share of the agreed-upon contract. If the option to buy or sell is exercised by the purchaser of an options contract, the shares must be bought or sold at the strike price. When you look at options online, the strike price is given at the end of the options symbol. For example, you might see:

00040000

The decimal point is found by moving three places from the right. So, this represents a strike price of $40.

00005600

It would represent a strike price of $5.60.

Time Value

How long is left until an options contract expires? Generally, more time value will mean that an option is worth more when trading. The reason is that the more time until the option expires, the more chance there is for the underlying stock to beat the strike price. In the case of a call option that means going above the strike price, while in the case of a put option that means going below the strike price. What investors are looking for is enough time value for an option to be in the money.

Time Decay

Time decay is simply a measure of the decrease in the time value of an options contract.

Underlying

The underlying stock is the specific stock that the option contract is based on. This is the stock that is traded if the option is exercised.

Weekly

A weekly is a kind of option that expires within a week, rather than a monthly time frame. Since weekly's have a short time value, they are cheaper, but the risks involved are higher. Investors who like weekly's are hoping to capitalize on an option that tightly fits a given date coming up soon. Weeklies usually expire on Friday afternoons at market close. Weeklies help traders that are trying to exploit short term events for profits. For example, investors might target an earnings report or an anticipated product announcement.

Chapter 6: Trading Strategies

While it can be easy to feel as though there is too much information out there regarding options trading to ever hope to keep it straight, there are several key strategies you will regularly use that you can focus on at the start to make the entire process far more manageable. As long as you take the time to utilize them correctly, you will find that each of the strategies outlined below will dramatically improve your success rate while decreasing your overall risk at the same time.

Keep in mind that the strategies that you use aren't nearly as important as the fact that you choose strategies that suit your trading style and compliments the trading plan you are focused on using for the time being. Keep in mind that just because a strategy seems useful doesn't mean it is going to be useful in your hands.

Married Put

Details: A married put is a great strategy if you have reason to take a bullish attitude towards the price of a given underlying asset while, at the same time, aiming to shore up any potential losses you might come across. To use this strategy properly, the first thing you will need to do is to purchase any amount of the underlying asset in question while simultaneously purchasing a put that covers the same amount. This will act as the price floor that will help you to prevent serious, unexpected losses in the case of a sudden price drop.

While the married put will not be the best choice in any situation, if used in the right way and with plenty of caution, it can be a reliable way to improve your successful trading percentage favorably. To ensure this always works out in your favor, you will never want to begin a new transaction without having a clear understanding of the risk you are working with beforehand. You will then be able to factor in additional costs more easily and compare the total cost to the amount of risk you are going to mitigate as a result.

After that, all that's left is going to be doing the math and choosing the option that makes the most fiscal sense at the moment. What's more, married puts also help to reduce the risk potential when it comes to early options to exercise as it ensures you always have available shares waiting in the wings.

Bull Call Spread

Details: To utilize the bull call spread successfully, you will want to start with a call option that can be purchased at a strike price that is worth returning to in the future. You will also need to sell an equal number of calls at a strike price that is above the initial strike price yet still within a reasonable distance. Both of these calls will also need to include the same timeframe as well as the same underlying asset. This is an excellent strategy to use if you feel bullish on the strength of the asset in question, or you have research that shows the price is likely to increase during your chosen timeframe.

This strategy also goes by the name vertical credit spread, thanks to its mismatched legs. Those that sell close to the money result in a credit spread that includes a positive time value and a net credit. Debit spreads are created if a short option ends further away from the money than the point it started from. Regardless, you can consider this strategy a net buy.

Bear Put Spread

Details: Similar in practice to the bull call spread, the bear put spread is useful under opposite circumstances. To use it effectively, you will need to purchase a pair of put options that have different strike prices, own lower and one higher. You will then need to purchase an equal number with the same timeframe and the same underlying asset. This can be an especially useful strategy if you have a bearish opinion of the underlying asset in question as it will help to limit your losses if you judge the market incorrectly. It is still important to be cautious, however, as the profits that it will bring you are always going to be limited to the difference between the two puts you initially purchased, minus any relevant fees.

The most profitable time to utilize this strategy is if you are already planning on short selling a specific underlying asset and a traditional put option won't provide you with the protection you need. You will likely find them especially useful if you plan on speculating and also feel that prices are going to decrease. This will allow you to avoid employing additional capital while only waiting for the worst to happen. As such, you will be able to hope for the best and plan for the worst at the same time.

Protective Collar

Details: The protective collar strategy can be executed by buying into a put option that is already out of the money. After that, you will then be able to create a secondary call option that is based on the same underlying asset that is also out of the money. Thus, this strategy is useful if you are already committed to a long position on an underlying asset that has a history of strong gains. Using a protective collar properly then allows you to ensure that you can anticipate a steady level of profit while also retaining control of the underlying asset if the positive trend does continue.

Straddle

Details: The straddle can be used to either go long or short. The long straddle can be extremely effective if you feel as though the price of a given underlying asset is going to move significantly in one direction; you just don't know what direction that will ultimately be. To utilize this strategy, you will need to purchase a put and a call, both using the same underlying asset, strike price, and timeframe. After the long straddle has been created successfully, you will be guaranteed to generate a profit if the price in question moves in either direction before it expires.

Strangle

Details: Functionally, a strangle is similar to a straddle except that it is often cheaper to execute on as you are buying into options that are already out of the money. As such, you can typically pay as much as 50 percent of the cost of a straddle for a strangle, which makes it even easier to play both sides of the fence. Typically, a long strangle is more useful than a short straddle because it offers up twice the premium for the same amount of risk.

To use the long strangle correctly, you will want to purchase a call along with a put that is both based on the same underlying asset with the same timeframe and different strike prices. The strike price for the call will need to be above the strike price for the put, and both should be out of the money. This strategy can be especially useful if you plan on the underlying asset moving a great deal without having a clear idea as to the direction. When used properly, this will virtually ensure you turn a profit once you have taken any fees out of the equation.

Butterfly Spread

Details: A butterfly spread is a combination of a bear spread and a traditional bull strategy that uses a total of three strike points. To begin with, you will need to purchase a call option at the lowest point you can manage before selling a pair of calls at a higher price and then a third call that has an ever-higher price. Your end goal with these purchases is to make sure that you have a range of prices you can profit from when everything is said and done.

This strategy can prove particularly effective when you have a completely neutral opinion on the current market. What's more, you should also expect the underlying asset to move in the direction that favors you, even if you don't have all the details locked down just yet. This then means that you will want to strive to keep the market volatility as low as possible. The greater the overall level of volatility, the greater the cost of this strategy will be. Furthermore, it is extremely important to keep in mind that if you choose incorrectly when it comes to the direction the underlying asset is going to move, then the amount you stand to lose can be significant.

Iron Condor

Details: To utilize the iron condor strategy, you will need to begin by taking a short position as well as a long position via a pair of strangles that is situated so they will take full advantage of a market that has staunchly low volatility. The pair of strangles should include both a long and a short, with both sets to the outer strike price. You can accomplish the same general effect with a pair of credit spreads if you are so inclined. In this scenario, the call spread would be placed above the market price, and the put would be placed beneath the current market price.

Iron Butterfly

Details: The iron butterfly strategy can be anchored by either a short straddle or a long straddle, depending on your needs. Regardless, you will want to then orchestrate a strangle based on the straddle you needed to use. The iron butterfly utilizes a mixture of puts and calls to limit the potential for loss (but also profits) around the strike price you formerly determined. This strategy is best used with options that are out of the money as they allow you to minimize both risk and cost.

ROI or Return on Investment

The Term ROI stands for Return on Investment. ROI is a measure of performance and is used by both investors and traders to measure the effectiveness and efficiency of an investment. This includes your trading capital. ROI deliberately endeavors to measure directly the total return derived from a particular investment.

For instance, if you invest a total of X amount on a particular trade and then received a return of Y from this investment, then ROI will endeavor to indicate the performance of your investment amount and what you received for your efforts. If you want to calculate the rate of return of an investment, you will need to know the total return, which is then divided by the investment amount.

One of the most important aspects of your investment portfolio is its profitability. You need to regularly monitor your investments, which are best achieved using the ROI or return on investment. It is advisable to work out what each dollar invested has generated. There is a formula for working out this figure.

R.O.I = (Profits − Costs) / Costs

Even then, investors need to understand that the ROI depends on numerous other factors such as the kind of investment security preferred and so on. Also, note that a high ROI implies higher risk, while a lower figure means reduced risk. For this reason, appropriate risk management must be undertaken.

Chapter 7: At the Money, Out of the Money, In the Money

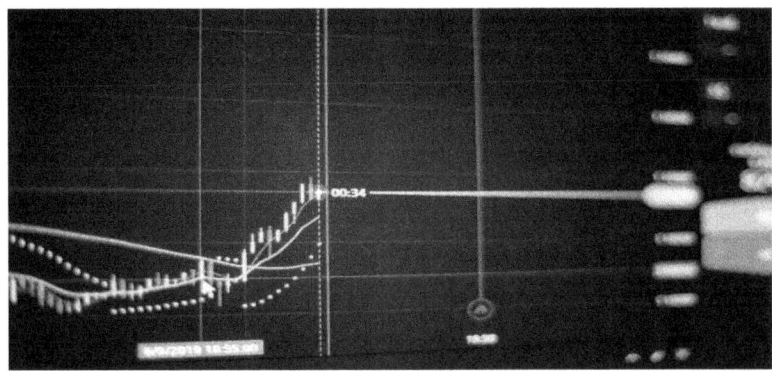

An option contract's worth changes dependent on the cost of the advantage basic it, for example, a stock, trade exchanged reserve, or fates contract. The alternative can be in cash (ITM), out of the cash (OTM), or at the cash (ATM). Every last one of these circumstances influences the inherent estimation of the alternative.

The measure of time staying before the choice agreement lapses additionally assumes a job in the estimation of choice, which like this influences how high or low a value—the premium—the purchaser is eager to pay for the choice.

In the Money

If an alternative agreement is ITM, it has characteristic worth. A call choice—which gives the purchaser the privilege however not the commitment to buy a benefit at a set cost before a specific day—is in the cash if the present cost of the fundamental resource is higher than that settled upon value, which is known as a strike cost. The purchaser could practice their privilege under the choice agreement and purchase the hidden resource for not as much as its present worth. That implies the call has inherent worth.

On the other hand, a put choice—which gives the purchaser the option to sell a benefit at a set cost at the latest a specific day—is ITM if the cost of the fundamental security is lower than the strike cost. The purchaser could practice their privilege under the alternative agreement and sell the basic resource for more than its present worth. That implies the put has inherent worth.

In outline, a call alternative is a wagered that the basic resource will ascend in cost at some point previously or on a specific day—known as the termination date—while a put choice is a bet that the basic resource's cost will fall during that period.

If the strike cost of a call choice is $5 and the basic stock is at present exchanging at $6, the alternative is ITM. The higher above $5 the cost goes, the more ITM the choice is and the more noteworthy its characteristic worth.

On the off chance that the strike cost of a put alternative is $5 and the fundamental stock is at present exchanging at $4, the choice is ITM. The lower beneath $5 the cost goes, the more ITM the choice is, and the more prominent its inborn worth.

The natural estimation of an alternative that is ITM is the more prominent of the strike cost or the cost of the basic resource less than the other cost. Along these lines, the characteristic incentive for both the call and put alternatives with the strike cost of $5 is $1.

Out of the Money

On the off chance that a choice agreement is OTM, it doesn't have natural worth. A call choice is OTM if the present cost of the fundamental resource is lower than the strike cost. The purchaser of the call choice would not practice their privilege under the choice agreement to purchase the basic resource since they would be paying more than its present worth.

Then again, a put choice is OTM if the present cost of the fundamental security is higher than the strike cost. The purchaser of the put choice would not practice their privilege under the alternative agreement to sell the fundamental resource since they would get not as much as its present worth.

On the off chance that the strike cost of a call choice is $5 and the basic stock is at present exchanging at $4, the alternative is OTM. The lower underneath $5 the cost goes, the more OTM the choice is.

On the off chance that the strike cost of a put choice is $5 and the basic stock is at present exchanging at $6, the choice is OTM. The higher above $5, the more OTM the alternative is.

Since these OTM put and call choices cannot be practiced for a benefit, their natural worth is zero.

At the Money

If an alternative agreement's strike cost is equivalent to the cost of the fundamental resource, the choice is ATM. On the off chance that the strike cost of a call or put choice is $5 and the basic stock is presently exchanging at $5, the alternative is ATM. Since ATM put and call alternatives cannot be practiced for a benefit, their characteristic worth is additionally zero.

Time Value

The estimation of choice comprises both inborn worth and time esteem. The more prominent the measure of time until a choice terminates, the additional time esteem it has. That is because there is a more noteworthy possibility the choice will, sooner or later, become ITM over the more drawn-out time allotment before termination thus has natural worth.

When choosing the amount of a top-notch they're willing to pay, a forthcoming alternative purchaser must contemplate whether the fundamental resource has or is probably going to have natural worth and the choice's time esteem. An alternative can be OTM and this way have no natural esteem yet, at the same time, have to time an incentive up until its termination. If an ITM choice has $10 of inborn worth, the premium ought to be higher than $10 given the time esteem characteristic in the measure of time the basic resource needs to turn out to be much more ITM.

Chapter 8: Volatility in the Markets

What is Volatility in the Markets?

Probably the greatest error and money washouts for starting poker players is playing an excessive number of hands. These players will in general like the "activity" and are not knowing enough about when a hand should be played or dropped.

The master player, then again, plays just when he finds the chances fundamentally in support of himself. He may change his style as indicated by different parts in the game (free versus tight; master versus novice, and so on) notwithstanding, by and large, he won't put his money in the "pot" except if he feels that there is a valid justification to do as such. He realizes that at last the cards will turn in support of himself and better hands will come up to give him his best playing openings.

This is the equivalent for the dealer. Starting traders are ordinarily energized, needing to engage in the "move." Positions are taken without satisfactory arranging. The expert option broker doesn't get included without having the option to acquire a critical chance. He examines option instability levels, the specialized example of the market, the pattern of the market, and the market's present response to a major news to decide if unpredictability is high, low or there are incongruities in option premium. He at that point chooses the best trading strategy to exploit both the instability levels and the specialized example and plans his exchange in like manner.

If there is no significant advantage or trading opportunity, he will stand aside.

He knows there will be different days and different business sectors that will give him "better playing hands".

That implies you should realize what is happening in the underlying business sector just as in the option market.

Once more, this is like playing poker. Three experts are for the most part thought to be an awesome hand. Nonetheless, in a circumstance where there are numerous different parts in the "pot" wagering firmly, it very well may be the correct move to discard that hand. Not playing marginal hands, and not trading in wrong circumstances are presumably the two most significant things new poker players and traders should learn.

After investigating the specialized example of the market, you at that point inspect option instability levels. We want to take a gander at "near" instability levels, positioning business sectors on a 1-10 scale contingent on their current "suggested" unpredictability levels, comparative with periods before.

At that point, you consolidate the relative unpredictability level with the specialized example of the underlying business sector to decide if an "extraordinary condition" or "positive circumstance" exits. You can fundamentally build your likelihood of benefit and additionally hazard/reward proportion by buying/selling either an option or a mix of options ("Option Spread Strategy").

This data is of such basic significance that its legitimate use can now and again permit us to be mistaken in our market perspectives and still be fruitful; while inappropriate use, (for example, purchasing extravagant, out-of-the-money options) can prompt misfortunes in any event, when the market moves altogether in support of yourself!

The accompanying frameworks all the trades that you consider for the diverse unpredictability levels. (This data is aimed at the off-floor dealer. Floor traders can utilize these situations in addition to other, more "exchange" type positions due to their speed of execution and low trading costs. Floor traders will in general utilize many "Delta Neutral" positions to press out premium from options on a momentary premise. This incorporates not just the "Unbiased Option Position" and "Proportion Spreads," which are our most loved ("Delta Neutral") positions, however, positions coordinating fates and options in practically any design to give them a bit of leeway including "boxes," "transformations" and so forth)

Coming up next are the lone positions you use in your trading portfolio 99% of the time:

1. NEUTRAL OPTION POSITION - High-medium option volatilities/trading range market (sell out-of-the-money put and out-of-the-money call in a similar expiration month). The "Nonpartisan Option Position" is best utilized in business sectors that have amazingly high premium (by selling out of sight the-money options), and trading range markets at any instability level that have little probability of huge development.

2. FREE TRADE - Low option instability exchange/moving business sector (purchase near the-money call or put, and if the market moves toward the path planned, later sell a lot farther of-the-money call or put at a similar price). The "Streamlined commerce" is utilized in moving business sectors to buy options of low to medium instability that are near the money (especially on pullbacks or responses against the pattern), and farther of-the-money options which can have a lot higher unpredictability levels are sold on meetings to finish the "Deregulation."

3. RATIO OPTION SPREAD - The premium difference between option strike prices, high unpredictability in out-of-the-money options/gently moving business sector (purchasing near-the-money option and selling at least two farther-of-the-money options). The "Proportion Spread" is utilized when dissimilarity in option premium exists. This, by and large, happens in amazingly high instability markets, for example, those that happen in silver and soybeans during meetings. For this situation, the near-the-money option is bought and at least two

further of-the-money options which can have up to twice as high option unpredictability levels are sold.

4. CALENDAR OPTION SPREAD - Premium uniqueness between option months, high unpredictability in near expiration options (offer near expiration month, purchase conceded month in a similar market). The "Schedule Option Spread" is utilized to exploit inconsistencies in unpredictability between various agreement months of a similar option. The pattern isn't as huge for this situation as long as we feel the option we sell will likely not be "in-the-money" at expiration.

5. IN-THE-MONEY-DEBIT SPREAD - The premium difference between strike prices/moving business sector (purchase in-the-money, or at-the-money option and sell farther of-the-money option). The "In-The-Money-Debit Spread" is started in unstable business sectors that are moving. Once more, like the "proportion spread," the at-the-money option which is all the more genuinely esteemed is bought and the farther of-the-money "exaggerated" option is sold.

6. NO-COST OPTION - Higher option instability in out-of-the-money options/exploit solid specialized help and opposition levels (purchase close to money option, sell out of the money put and call). The "No Cost Option" permits us to buy an option with the exceptional we get from selling another option premium to pay for it.

That is, it and that is everything that matters. You might need to utilize different positions yourself, you might need to create muddled multi-legged positions, yet I have discovered these to be the solitary reliably viable ones that can be practically utilized and give a critical bit of leeway. It is instability that chooses whether options are high or low priced. (Most different books and experts generally allude to these as "exaggerated" and "underestimated" options). We accept that this can be a hazardous misnomer and the reason for pointless misfortunes for traders.

How Option Volatility Determines Which Option Strategy to Use

At the point when I originally began trading, I saw that analysts and brokers would frequently suggest a vertical bull spread if the market was going up and a bear vertical spread if the market was going down. Their thinking was that if the market acted as they anticipated, this position would bring in money.

Nonetheless, they seldom gave explanations behind utilizing these systems, nor was there any conversation of how this position would give the broker an "edge" over a net future or option position.

Indeed, when there is no specific motivation to utilize these techniques, (for example, uniqueness in option premium), this position would be averse to the dealer given both slippage and commissions in entering and leaving this position. What's more, benefits would be restricted if the market moved generously in the broker's courtesy.

Additionally, except if the broker dissected the entirety of the volatilities of the diverse strike prices of each option month, the merchant could undoubtedly be buying an "exaggerated" option.

Our prerequisite while starting any option position is that we can get some kind of "edge" because of either low unpredictability when buying options, high instability when selling options, or a difference in option expenses when consolidating the two.

At the point when fates or values broker chooses to take a position, he needs just decide the heading he is anticipating the market will move by investigating central and specialized information and the price level he wishes to start his position. Nonetheless, this isn't the situation in options trading (although this is all that many starting option traders use). As we have talked about, there are ordinarily where you could purchase an option, have the market move toward the path you anticipated, and still lose money Additionally, there are other unfavorable variables of option trading including a lot of lower liquidity, causing slippage in both entering and leaving the position.

Hence, to try not to be dependent upon the impeding parts of trading options and be in a situation to profit from the huge preferences accessible by utilizing the qualities of option techniques, the option broker should work a lot harder and be more educated. He should not just dissect similar elements vital for net prospects or values position (i.e., course and passage and leave focuses), yet besides, should be learned about utilizing option instability. The broker should know whether instability is moderately high or low, the best strike prices, month, and techniques that exploit option estimating incongruities.

How Option Volatility Can Alert You in Advance to Significant Market Moves

At the point when option instability is at low levels, there is a high likelihood that a huge move is going to happen. It appears to be that when an agreement is exceptionally calm, traders apparently "nod off" and don't anticipate that anything should occur. This is actually when everything detonates! Then again, ordinarily, when the market has been dynamic (unpredictable) for a while since most traders are as of now on the lookout, it is probably going to keep a trading range. Be that as it may, understanding this idea of unpredictability is a lot simpler than utilizing it in trading.

The new option trader regularly dismisses unpredictability. He decides just that a market is moving a specific way and buys an option that best accommodates his perspective available and danger introduction. This trader will lose when the market moves against his ideal heading or stays nonpartisan. He will likewise regularly lose, in any event, when the market moves toward him, as a result of the time rot of the estimation of the option premium.

The proficient option trader will analyze the instability of the option contract and decide if it's in the high, low, or center of its verifiable reach.

He will at that point assess the diverse strike price and long stretches of options, and not just pick the option or strategy that furnishes him with an "edge."

For instance, the call option buys furnished situations with a magnificent danger/reward proportion in silver and the grains in mid-1993. The options had low unpredictability joined with dependable specialized graph design which recommended that there was a solid likelihood of a breakout to the potential gain.

The contrary picture was clear in the bond options in late 1993. A trader who might have bought any out-of-the-money options would have lost money since the market stayed in a trading range. The entirety of the out-of-the-money options, the two puts, and calls, lost an incentive during this period. Consequently, it didn't make a difference in this market whether you were bullish or bearish. All purchasers of options weren't right, all vendors were correct.

Perceiving these standards isn't just significant in deciding the most ideal option strategy to utilize, yet also, can make you aware of likely alters in the course of the underlying business sector.

Chapter 9: Options Pricing

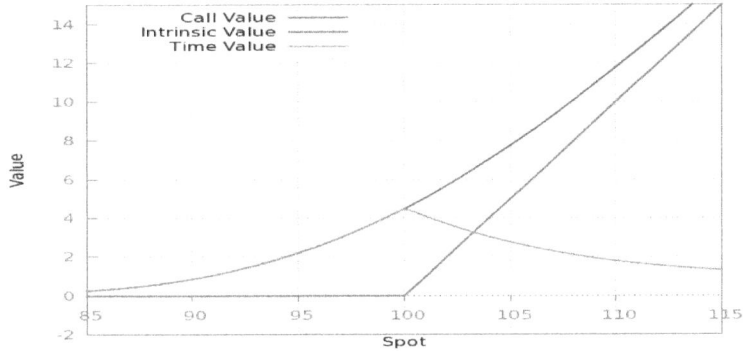

Options prices are determined in part by the price of the underlying stock. But options prices are also influenced by the time left to expiration and other factors. We are going to go over all the different ways that the price of a given option can change and what will be behind the changes. It is important to have a firm grasp of these concepts so that you do not go into options as a naïve beginning trader.

Market Price of Shares

The largest factor that impacts the price of an option is the price of the investment known as the stock that is behind the option. However, it's not a 1-1 relationship. The amount of influence from the underlying stock changes with time. Furthermore, it depends on whether the option is in the money, at the money, or out of the money. The fraction of the options price that is due to the price of the underlying stock is called the option's *intrinsic value*.

If an option is the same as the market pricing or not be comparatively favored, it has no intrinsic value. An option has to be priced in the money to have an intrinsic value.

For a call option, if the market price is lower than the strike price or the same, the option will have no value intrinsically. If the share price is higher than the price used to trade shares via the option, the option will have intrinsic value.

For a put option, if the share price is at or above the strike price, the option will have no intrinsic value. If the share price is below the strike price, then the option will have intrinsic value.

However, even when an option is out or at the money, the worth of the underlying stock has around the impact that can alter the worth of the option. The quantity of influence that the market price of the stock has on the price of the option is given by a quantity that is called *delta*. Delta is given as a decimal value ranging from 0 to 1 for call options. It is given as a negative value for put options. The reason for the negative value for put options is that this reflects the fact that if the stock price is found to increase, the price of a put option will be reduced. In contrast, if the stock price declines, the value of the put option will increase. It is an inverse relationship, and thus, the delta is negative for put options.

To understand how this will play out, let's look at a specific example. Suppose that we have a $100 option. That is, the strike price is set to $100. If the price of the underlying stock is $105, the delta for the call option is $0.77.

If the dollar value of the stock increases by $1, the value of the option will increase by around $0.77. It is a per-share price change. For an option that trades 100 underlying shares, a $0.77 price rise will increase the value of the option by $77.

For a put option with the same strike price, the option will be out of the money because the share price is higher than the strike price. In the case of the put option, the delta is -0.23. The put option will lose approximately $23 if the share price went up by $1. On the other hand, if the share price drops by $1, the put option will gain $23.

The intrinsic value of the call option described in this theoretical exercise is $5 per share. The total cost of the option is $6.06 per share, reflecting the fact that the call option has $1.06 in extrinsic value. In contrast, the put option has no intrinsic value. It has almost the same extrinsic value, however, at $1.03.

I used a 45-day time frame before expiration for this exercise. Options prices are governed by mathematical formulas, so it is possible to make estimates of what the option price is going to be ahead of time. There are many calculators and spreadsheets available free online for this purpose.

Now, let's say that instead, the share price is $95 so that the call option will be out of the money and the put option is in the cash. In this case, the call option has no intrinsic value, and it has a $0.94 extrinsic value. Therefore, the option would be worth $94. In this case, the delta is 0.25. If the share price rose to $96, with everything else unchanged, the price of the call option would rise to $1.21 per share. This illustrates that you can still earn profits from cheaper out of the money options.

If the share price stays at $95, the put option will have a delta of -0.75. Notice that if we take the absolute value and add the delta for the call and the put option, they sum up to 1.0.

If a call option has a strike that is lower than the market price and has a delta of 0.8, the put option with the same strike price and expiration date will have a delta of -0.20.

Delta does more than give you the prediction of changes in the underlying share price and price movements of the option. It also gives a rough estimate of the probability of an option to expire in the money. If you sell to open, you do not want the option to expire in the money. Therefore, you are probably going to sell options that have a small delta. On the other hand, if you buy to open, you want the option to go in the money, if it is not already. So, you would buy an option with a higher delta.

If a given call option has a delta of 0.66, this indicates that if the underlying stock price rises by $1, the price of the option on a per-share basis will rise by $0.66. It also tells us that there is a 66% chance that this option will expire in the money.

Something else you need to know is that the delta is dynamic. If the price of a share increases on the market, the delta rises for the call option and gets smaller for the put option. A declining share price will have contradictory consequences.

The amount that delta will change is given by another Greek called the gamma. Most beginner traders probably are not going to be too worried about gamma. What we have described so far is all you need to know to enter into effective options trades. But gamma will tell you the variation in the value of the delta with a change in stock price. So, if gamma is 0.03, this means that a $1 rise in the stock price will increase delta by 0.03 for a call option. The inverse relationship holds for a put option.

If an option is at the money, the delta is going to be about 0.50 for a call option and -0.50 for a put option. That makes sense as if the strike price is equal to the share price on the market, there is a 50% probability that the market price will move below the strike price, and there is a 50% probability that the market cost of shares will move above the strike price.

Implied Volatility

One of the most important characteristics of options after considering delta and time decay is the amount a stock price varies with time. Volatility will give you an idea of how wide the price swings of stock are. If you look at a stock chart, you will see the price go up and down a lot giving a largely jagged curve. The more that it fluctuates and the bigger the fluctuations in price, the higher the volatility. Everything is relative and so, you can't say that any stock has an absolute level of volatility. The volatility of a stock is compared to the volatility of the market as a whole. This quality is called beta.

If the stock generally moves with the stock market at large, beta is positive. A 1.0 beta means that stock has the same volatility as the market. This is a stock with average volatility.

If beta is less than 1.0, then the stock is less volatile than the market. An amount below 1.0 tells you how much less volatile the stock is in comparison to the market as a whole. If the beta is 0.7, this means that the stock is 30% less volatile than the market average.

If beta is greater than 1.0, then the stock is more volatile than the average. If you see a stock with a beta of 1.42, this means the stock is 42% more volatile than the average of the market.

If beta is negative, the stock moves against the market. When the market goes up, it goes down and vice versa. Most stocks do not have a negative beta but they are not hard to find either.

Volatility is a dynamic quantity, so when you look it up, you are looking at a snapshot of the volatility at that given moment. Of course, under most circumstances, it's not likely to change very much over short periods. There are exceptions to this, including earnings season.

Implied volatility is another quantity that is given to options. Implied volatility is a measure of the coming volatility that the stock price is expected to see over the lifetime of the option. That is, until the expiration date.

One of the things that make options valuable is the probability that the price of the stock will move in a direction that is favorable to the strike price. When an option goes in the money, or moves even higher relative to the strike price of a call, or lower relative to the strike price of a put, the value of the option can increase by a large margin.

More volatile stocks have a higher chance of this happening. This is a result of the price working through greater price swings. Consequently, the higher the implied volatility, the higher the price of the option.

Let's consider a hypothetical situation to illustrate. This time, we will look at an option that would have a strike price that was set to $100 and $100 share price. The option is at the money. Here are the prices that you will see for different values of implied volatility:

- Implied volatility = 40%: Option price is $562.
- Implied volatility = 20%: Option price is $282
- Implied volatility = 10%: Option price is $142
- Implied volatility = 80%: Option price is $1,119

That is for a call option.

As you can see, implied volatility has quite a large influence on the price of an option. For this reason, professional options traders look at implied volatility just as much as they look at the comparison between the strike price and the market stock price. One way to make profits is to seek out options that have higher implied volatility.

Each quarter, companies report their earnings. This is a time when implied volatility is really important. As mentioned earlier, earnings calls can fluctuate the price of a stock up or down by large amounts. Prices can move in one direction or the other depending on whether the earnings call beat expectations or not. This also depends on whether or not there is good or bad news thrown in with the earnings report. This is a highly volatile situation indeed!

This offers opportunities for profits. Many professional traders handle this by purchasing options on companies that will have upcoming earnings calls. Typically, this purchase is made about a week ahead of the earnings call. At that time, the implied volatility is going to be relatively low. It may be in the range of 15-20%.

As time passes and it gets closer to the earnings call, implied volatility will go up by a lot. In fact, for the examples above it was no accident that I selected implied volatility of 80%. Recently, I noticed that the implied volatility on some Tesla options shot up to 82%. As implied volatility goes up, the value of the option increases. This provides an opportunity for profits.

Time Decay

The time until expiration has a great influence on the worth of an option. If an option is valued so that it is the same as the share price, or if it is out of the money, time decay is going to have a significant influence over the value of an option at any given time. For an option that is in the money, the influence of time decay is much less. The closer the expiration date gets; the less influence time value has on the overall price of the option.

In such a case, the option is more influenced by implied volatility and the underlying share price. For example, an option with a 4-day expiration date, a $100 strike price on an underlying stock when the market price is equal to $110 per share will have $10 in intrinsic value with $0.56 in extrinsic value and a total price per share of $10.56. The price is heavily weighted to the underlying price of the shares. However, theta is -0.23, meaning that on a per-share basis, at market open the following day, the option will lose $0.23 in value, all other things being equal. Of course, all other things are not equal, and changes in share price and implied volatility may wipe that out or add to it.

The important thing to do is check theta every afternoon so you can estimate what the cost is going to be for holding the option overnight. Time decay is an exponential phenomenon, so decay occurs faster the closer you get to the expiration date. The important fact to remember is that when other factors are going to be more important than time decay, do not simply sell the option because it is going to lose value from time decay the following morning.

Risk-Free Rate

The risk-free rate quoted for an option is the interest rate that you can earn on an ideal safe investment. Generally speaking, this is the interest you can earn on a 10-year U.S. treasury over the time of the option. In normal times, this is an important factor to consider. Rising interest rates can lower the value of options. In recent years, interest rates have been very low and changes in interest rates have been small and very conservative.

Chapter 10: Advanced Trading Strategies

The goal in options trading is to earn profits by analyzing stock charts and trends in the securities market. Once you are good at analyzing the market and finding the right time to enter and exit, you will be earning money as well as gaining experience. More skill, knowledge, and experience will then limit the amount of risk you bear when making your options trading activities.

While advanced trading strategies are good, you need to make sure that you understand the strategy before applying it. If you are a beginner options trader, starting with the basics is very important. Seek to gain mastery over the market when you are feeling bullish, bearish, and neutral about the stock price movements in the market.

It is also very important that you expand your brokerage account to be able to use some of these advanced trading strategies while trading in options. A demo trading level is good to seek trial before signing up for a brokerage account. Once you are okay with how the brokerage account, sign up for the basic level. Success at using the basic trading strategies to make money should then take you to the next level in your options trading plan: advanced options trading.

When it comes to using advanced trading strategies, one of the most important things to consider is analysis. Your analysis is what determines the kind of strategy to use. Through technical and fundamental analysis, you can make predictions in the market to determine when things will be bullish, bearish, and neutral. These forecasts come with their corresponding plans, which should go to build upon your trading.

Combining Fundamental and Technical Analysis for Advanced Trading

While you may choose to prefer one method of analysis much more than the other, the most important thing is always to learn how to can blend or combine the two analytical approaches on the stock market to make a good trading decision.

Maybe you have been looking at a stable and liquid stock that has not been experiencing much volatility in the stock market. All of a sudden, the stock begins to fluctuate in the market. Instead of jumping and making your trading decisions, you must stay objective and adopt both a technical and fundamental analysis to make a well-informed decision.

In some cases, volatility in a stock market can be influenced by changes in the micro and macro-economic conditions of the company. When these factors change, they tend to impact revenue, stock per earnings, dividends, interest rates, and certainly stock movement. This is the reason some schools of thought say you should never take any real money position in the market if you have not used technical and fundamental analysis to make an informed forecast in the stock market.

How Fundamental and Technical Analysis Complements Each Other

There are different kinds of traders in the market. The information required from each trader to decide on the market may vary from one to another. That means looking at what the market forecasts and financial news media are saying and then checking whether the information agrees with each other.

The goal is to make a bullish technical analysis that has a strong confirmation from a fundamental analysis perspective. If the stock appears bullish from a technical perspective, but then weak from the technical analysis, you might want to watch and consider your decision and forecasts. To generate profitable trades and to ensure that the tides are moving in your favor, you have to ensure that there is an agreement between your technical analysis forecasts and fundamental analysis forecasts.

This will help increase the probability of your decisions being correct and earning you revenue with each trading activity. A good 50/50 outlook from a technical analysis and fundamental analysis perspective can help increase your winning trades and ensure your trading capital has not been wiped out. Therefore, always learn to pair or combine the analytic reports of both sides when making your options trading decision.

Analytical Trading Example

- Revenue Earning Seasons

At the end of every quarter, all publicly traded companies are required by law to provide a report on their quarterly performance. Before their reports, there is some level of market predictions based on their performance for the past quarter. This quarterly information provided by the company gives a deep insight into the status of the company financially, and its capability to yield profit and increase earnings per share.

When the final quarterly financial reports are provided by the company, and the market realizes that the results have beaten market expectations, the difference in expectation tends to lead to an increase in stock prices, causing a change in the financial charts. As a seasoned trader looking to excel in capital gains, you have to analyze the financial reports of the company and the market reactions to help determine whether stock prices will move upward or downward. This can help you know whether to feel bullish, bearish, or neutral about the market.

- Catastrophic Events

The stock price of a company can be affected by catastrophic events occurring in the company. Assuming a publicly-traded company has been poorly managed by the directors and officers of the company leading some of their subsidiaries to go bankrupt or close, it will affect their stock price. The stock price of a company is likely to go down if they have a huge lawsuit that has resulted in the company being fined hundreds and millions of dollars by the court system.

As a technician, you need to keep watch over this information and use them to make your trading decisions. Bankruptcies, lawsuits, poor management, and many other internal events were going on in a company go a long way to affect the earnings per stock and the general stock price of the company. This is why an advanced trading strategy involves blinding both fundamental and technical investing to trade.

- Global Economic Uncertainty

During times of global uncertainty, people tend to move their money from one financial instrument to another. In this case, the price of gold is inclined to rise when the global economy is uncertain. When companies are running into bankruptcies, and stock prices tend to be going down, people tend to move their funds to other asset classes such as silver and gold. When this happens, you need to analyze the market and then adjust your options trading plan to profit from the market changes.

- Economic Data Releases

There is an impact of economic data on the market. And this is very important for options traders to know whether cash is flowing from one asset class to another to increase prices on the economic data. The following are typical levels for which economic data are being released for trading activities:

- o Gross Domestic Product (GDP)
- o Retail Prices of Commodities
- o Consumer Inflation
- o Manufacturing Productivity
- o Unemployment Rate
- o Currencies

The news and information from these economic indicators have a way of affecting stock price movements. Companies are affected and influenced by the economic environment that they operate in. For example, an increase in the prices of commodities like oil can cause some companies to increase the price of their goods and services. This will impact the stock price, trends, and moods of the market.

Always be on the lookout for economic data and trend information. This information is very critical in determining stock trends. When things are tough, and the market gets hard, many people end up engaging in profit first decisions that ruin their lives. Understand success factors that lead to stock price movements and changes.

- Central Bank Meetings

Sometimes there can be an effect in stock prices with a change in interest rates. This can be influenced by the meeting of stockholders of central banks. Decisions of central banks affect interest rates, import/export rates. Setting stock volume/benchmarks and market volatility.

Key central banks whose decisions play a big impact on the global market include the following: US Federal Reserve, the European Central Bank, the Bank of England, the People's Bank of China, the Bank of Japan, the Swiss National Bank, and the Bank of Australia.

Generally, an increase in interest rates will create a bearish effect on the market, which will decrease stock prices. In this case, the associated bearish strategies have to be adopted to ensure that the best trading results have been obtained.

The Bottom Line

From a fundamental analysis perspective arising through global economic uncertainty, options traders will begin to notice that the price of commodities like gold and silver will move upward. Option traders dealing in gold and silver can then feel bullish about the market and then adopt advanced bullish trading strategies to profit from the dynamic change in the market.

Many traders in the market use technical trading to realize profits in the market. But there are limitations to these approaches just as there are limitations to the fundamental approach. While there is no definite answer as to where the technical analysis should instead of fundamental analysis, the key is to make sure that you leverage both approaches to complement each other and make better trading decisions.

Advanced Trading Indicators

Once you develop your technical, analytical skills and find ways to predict the movement in the market accurately, you have to use a set of strategies to capitalize on that prediction. As you get into the advanced levels of your options trading, these trading methods will become familiar to you and enable you to make better profits with the trading capital at your disposal. Advanced technical indicators help you to know which of the trades meets your analysis and outlook on the market so that you can be able to generate profits.

The following are the top advanced technical indicators for options trading:

- Relative Strength Index
- Commodity Channel Index
- Stochastics
- Fibonacci retracements
- Debit Spreads
- Credit Spreads
- Butterfly Spreads

- Iron Condors

Commodity Channel Index (CCI)

If you are looking for trends in commodity prices, the best technical indicator to look out for is the Commodity Channel Index. The commodity channel index is a good technical tool for those who are trading in commodities. The key is to analyze stock price movements over some time. Usually, price ranges are marked from -100 to +100. When a commodity falls below -100, then it means it has been oversold. This will create a market strategy for call options. The reverse will create a suitable market for put options.

Chapter 11: Strike Price

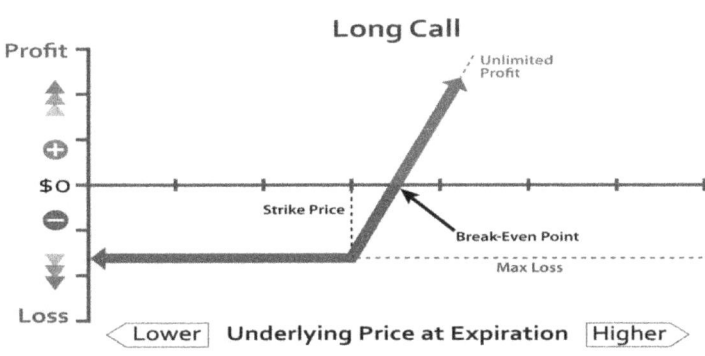

What is Strike Price?

The strike price is one of the most significant if not the most significant thing to comprehend when it comes to option contracts. The strike price will determine whether the underlying stock is bought or sold at or before the expiration date. When evaluating any options contract, the strike price is the first thing that you should look at. It's worth reviewing the concept and how it's utilized in the actual marketplace.

The strike price will let you home in on the profits that can be made on an options contract. It's the break-even point but also gives you an idea as to your profits and losses. Unquestionably, the seller at all times contracts the premium by hook or by crook.

Intended for a call contract, the strike price is the price that must be surpassed by the existing market price of the underlying equity. For example, if the strike price is $100 on a call contract, and the current market price goes to any price above $100, then the purchaser of the call can exercise their right at any time to buy the stock. Then the stock can be disposed of with a profit. Suppose that the current price rises to $130. Then you can exercise your option to buy the stock at $100 a share, and then turn around and sell it on the market for $130 a share, making a $30 profit per share before taking into account the premium and other fees that might accrue with your trades. While as the buyer of the contract you have no obligations other than paying the premium, the seller is obligated no matter what, and they must sell you the shares at $100 per share no matter how much it pains them to see the $130 per share price. Of course, there are reasons behind the curtain that will explain why they would bother entering this kind of arrangement that we will explore later. For a put contract, the strike price likewise plays a central role, but the value of the stock relative to the strike price works oppositely. A put is a bet that the underlying equity will decrease in value by a certain amount. Hence if the stock price drops below the strike price, then the buyer can exercise their right to sell the shares at the strike price even though the market price is lower. So, if your price is $100, if the current price of the equity drops to $80, the seller is obligated to buy the 100 shares per contract from you at $100 a share even though the market price is $80 per share. In this case, you've made a gross profit of $20 a share.

The value of the strike price will not only tell you profitability but give you an indication of how much the stock must move before you can exercise your rights. Often when the amount is smaller, you might be better off.

When you know the strike price of different options contracts, then you can evaluate which one is better for you to buy. Suppose that a stock is currently trading at $80 and you find two options put contracts. One has a strike price of $75 and the other has a strike price of $60. Further, let's suppose that both contracts expire at the same time. In the first case, the stock price in the market will need to drop just $5 before the contract becomes profitable. For the second contract, it will have to drop by $20. The potential worth of each contract per share is the difference. For the contract with the $75 strike price, that is only $5. For the second contract with the strike price of $60, the potential worth is $20, four times as much.

Determining which contract is better is a matter of analysis and taking some risk. You can't just go by face value, but you must take into consideration the expiration date together with an analysis of what the stock will do over that period. It may be that it's going to be impossible for the stock to drop $20 to make the second contract valuable. If the expiration date comes before the stock drops that much in price, the contract will be worthless. In other words, you'd never be able to exercise your option of selling shares at a striking amount. On the other hand, even though there is not much discrepancy between the strike and the market amount for the first contract, and the market price might only drop to say $70 per share, the chances of this happening before the expiration date is more likely.

Your analysis might be different if the contract with the lower strike price has a longer expiration date.

The lesson to take to heart is that a stock is more likely to move by smaller amounts over short periods. But the higher the risk, the more potential profits.

Chapter 12: Option Trader Mindset

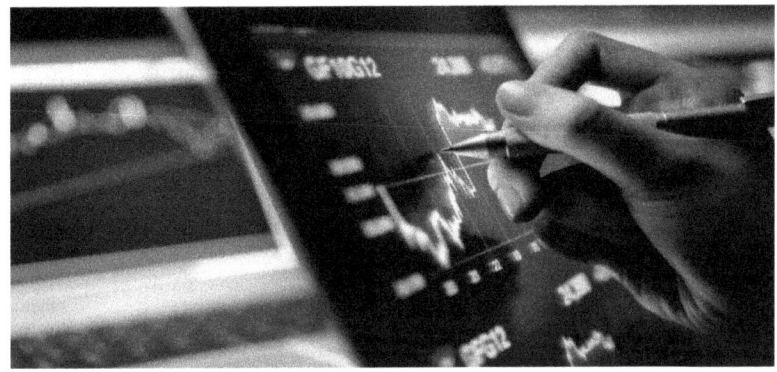

A successful options trader is a unique individual. This person learns how to leverage their financial position to pave a way to profitable returns that make the time and effort invested worth it. This person is strong-willed and determined.

I have tried to break down the concepts in this book as simple as possible so that anyone can do it. The truth is even though everyone can understand these concepts and maybe the ability to implement these strategies, not everyone has the fortitude to stick with it until they gain the results they want—which is financial freedom. The people that do, fall into a small bracket. A strong options trader requires a unique set of skills, attitude, and persona.

The Traits of a Successful Options Trader

- Being self-disciplined. I am sure after reading this book, you may be excited about the possibility of gaining financial freedom by using options trading. If you are willing to jump with both feet in, I applaud you. I also implore you to exercise caution and therefore, self-discipline. Do not just stop your education on options with this book. Do more extensive research so that you can identify the best opportunities for you. Doing this will allow you to form the best strategy for your case and goals. Do not skip doing your homework because you are eager. Jumping the gun has led to many traders losing out. You need to rule your desires, wants, and actions rather than being ruled by them.

- Being Committed. A successful options trader is one that does not give up. He or she does not trade on an on-again, off-again basis. This person is committed to the cause of building their financial success in this way and persists in their effort. Remember, I stated in the introduction of this book, that this is not a hobby. This is something you embrace as a business and part of your lifestyle. Go hard or go home. Options trading has no room for being tentative.

- Continually learning. The financial market is continuously evolving. It changes every single day. A successful trader needs to be able to roll with the punches and have a clear understanding of what is happening now. He or she needs to be able to make forecasts about the future as well. Continuously learning about the market also allows you to see new opportunities where amateur traders will not. One of the best ways to increase your knowledge of options is to follow the action of an experienced options trader. The point is not to copy his or her moves. Rather, it is to watch a master at work so that you can develop your style of trading.

- Being patient. This relates to jumping the gun. You need to carefully weigh your options before you make a move while trading options. While there are risks involved in trading options, the market typically provides signs of these opportunities if a trader knows where and how to look. Control your emotions and strategize your entry into the trade market as well as your exit from trades.

- Being an effective risk manager. There is no guarantee when you trade options and as such, an effective options trader needs to be able to exploit his or her position to try to determine where he or she should take appropriate measures to capitalize on his or her gain. Part of managing risks involves being able to diversify your portfolio so that all your eggs are not in one basket. A successful trader does not go chasing after every available option. Neither does he or she get stuck chasing China eggs that do not yield gain. Even though there is no guarantee that it will all work out, being able to effectively manage risks significantly lowers the chances of the loss happening.

- Being able to manage money effectively. The trader also needs to know how much capital should be allocated for trading. Throwing your money at all options will not lead to effective results. This is a recipe for losing money. Part of being a good money manager means the trader needs to be good with numbers so that he or she can calculate the Vega, theta, delta, and gamma of their trade options, for example.
- Maintaining accurate records. This will help with decision-making and allows you to allocate your money effectively as you will have a history of your options within easy reach. My suggestion is that you do this digitally for easy access, better storage, and better organization. Digitally record-keeping also allows for the use of specialized software that makes life a lot simpler than looking through hard copies when records are needed.
- Being an effective planner. While there is a level of relying on instinct in trading options, you also need to have a plan so you do not place random trades. You need to have the direction to effectively move forward with obtaining financial freedom no matter which option you choose to do that. Having smart goals allow you to develop this plan. You also need to have a plan to cover any losses that may happen and a plan for how you can leverage the profit that you do make. Your plan needs to allow for flexibility and the great thing is that you can upgrade, downscale, and change the plan completely if need be.

- Being able to accept losses gracefully. The nature of the financial market is unpredictable and every trader makes a loss at some point. Having an apt understanding of the market will minimize this loss but you also need to be able to be flexible in how you handle this so that you do not get blindsided nor do you let this weigh you down. Remember that any successful person needs to be able to find a lesson in their failure so that they come back stronger and better in the future.

Dream Big

Many people are stuck in a state of financial dependency and insecurity because they do not see themselves as being any better than they are now. Therefore, they never take any actions or risks to elevate themselves

You need to be able to visualize your success to manifest it. To develop yourself into a brilliant trader, you need to be able to see yourself in the future as a successful entrepreneur who implemented a plan to gain passive income and is, therefore, able to enjoy the freedom of using your time as you see fit.

The brain has a way of manifesting action to make what it sees a reality so use that to your advantage. See yourself as a successful options trader today. Imagine the way that you would look, the way that you would feel, how you would dress and everything else that being an options trader means to you. See yourself being more than what you are today no matter your current circumstances. Do not place any limits on yourself.

The mistake that many options traders make at the beginning is that they think small. They imagine maybe making a few hundred dollars here and there to subsidize their current lifestyle. They make that the pinnacle of their success even though many options traders make hundreds of thousands and millions of dollars every day.

The people that dream so small have their reasons but a common reason is that they do not want to be too disappointed if things do not work out. This way of thinking is limiting and self-fulfilling. You are stopping yourself from achieving greatness and reaching your true potential with such a mindset. Instead, you have to dream big, bold dreams. It is the only thing that will keep you motivated in tough times. You have to **know** that you can do this and make this a successful business no matter the odds.

I know that at the beginning, it may be tough especially when people laugh at your dreams of becoming a success. Remember that you are not doing this for them. Those people maybe your friends and family and of course, this hurt. Do not allow this to demotivate you. Keep strong and remember that you are doing this for yourself, not them. If you need to, make it an extra motivator to prove them wrong. Give yourself the last laugh.

Visualizing allows you to have something to work towards. The vision creates a hunger within you to manifest that picture in your mind into reality. It builds anticipation and creates excitement. It gives you a sense of purpose. Allow yourself to be consumed by that passion.

I believe that every person on this planet is capable of doing great things so stop limiting yourself. Stop underestimating your potential. One of the most significant attributes of an options trader is being able to follow his or her gut. You will never develop that knack for trading options if you continually doubt yourself and your purpose.

All of the traits that are stated above are things that can be learned. So, it is fine if you have not developed these traits as yet. The point is to make it a habit to develop them starting today. The first thing you need to do is picture yourself as the successful options trader that you will be in the future. Then put in the work to make that vision a reality.

Chapter 13: Buying and Selling Puts

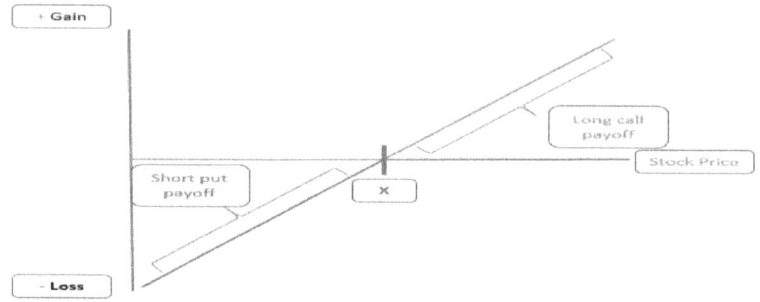

Buying Puts

Buying puts can be a winning strategy if done right. The stock market wouldn't be the stock market if it only moved in one direction. By buying puts as well as calls, you're making the most of the market by profiting no matter which direction it is heading. Puts are your ally during a bear market.

Buying a put means that you are going to make a profit with a stock declining in price. Just as you're looking for a stock to skyrocket in a call, you're looking for one that will plunge in a put. The strategy is, therefore, very similar and it's just that you're looking in the opposite direction.

Most traders buy puts both because they're speculating on stock, and think they can make a profit in the short term as that stock plummets, or because the puts can function as insurance for your overall portfolio. If you own the stock in question, you can buy puts on it if you believe it's at risk of heading downward.

For instance, let's say you own stock in a company and you think the share price will drop because of the business environment. You aren't sure, but you can make an educated guess. Simply leaving that stock sitting in your portfolio means potentially watching as its value bleeds away.

On the other hand, you could buy a put and give yourself the option to offload that stock if it does drop to a certain value. As the buyer, you are not obligated to sell your stock when the deadline arrives. You're just giving yourself the option to do so. Of course, as always, you'll lose the premium.

The biggest difference between buying calls and puts is that the stock market has a habit of falling much faster than it rises. A stock can drop through the floor in just a single day whereas it can take weeks or months to climb to magical figures.

To buy puts for the sake of speculation, you'll need to master the art of spotting weaker stocks—the ones that are likely to fall. That is easiest during a bear market and when the overall economic outlook is poor.

Even the most successful companies have downtimes and, if you own a put contract when that happens, you stand to make money.

When buying a put, you'll need to think in reverse. The lower the strike price, the cheaper the option will be. In other words, it is the opposite of buying a call. You should also factor in the speed of the market when looking at expiration dates. If you think the stock is going to drop hard and fast, you probably want a shorter deadline. If you think it will take a while for the full effects of the drop to realize, then you will want a longer one.

The most successful put strategies, at least at first, will probably be slightly in the money because you can profit from a smaller change in the underlying value. Conversely, you'll make more money on a smaller premium with an out of the money put but you have less chance of actually making that money.

Selling Puts

Selling puts can be a gamble. The idea behind it is that, by selling your promise to buy stocks, you are earning a steady premium but you're choosing contracts that you believe will never hit the strike price. That way, you walk away having been paid for the contract without having to own the underlying stock.

It's also a way to increase your stock portfolio and get paid for doing so. That can be useful if you think a stock's dropping price is temporary and you want to snap up a few of them before they start to rise again and you can sell them.

Be aware, of course, that when selling a put you are obligating yourself to buy that stock if it does reach the strike price, so, it's a bad gamble if you lack the funds to do that when the expiration date arrives.

Chapter 14: Passive Income

Hey, do you ever wonder how fun it would be earning money without actively working for it? Yes, there are opportunities like these. Imagine those shareholders who subscribe to those shares where they are not actively engaged in them. Therefore, passive income is a kind of business where you put much effort into ensuring its success. Remember that the opposite of this source of money is the active income which you have directly involved in the work. That is like the work you do for your company or shop.

Perhaps you are get fancied with this idea that you are getting money without struggling for it. Ever thought the plot or the land you have is a gold mine. Now you know because you can convert those properties to earn for you even when you are sleeping. Hey, it is not hard because here are the most unusual ways to make passive income.

First, you can lease your properties for rent, let your premises earn for you, do not have to be there all the time to supervise the building. The only cost you will incur is creating that building and furnishing it. However, the price will be compensated by the money those tenants pay either annually or monthly. You can even choose an agent who will monitor the premises for you. What you expect is the cash that the tenants pay.

You can be an online trader either in stocks or other securities without actively participating in it. Such action is called index funds, which are significant in trading without getting involved in it. Some of you may wonder how that can be possible. Think if you invest in an index fund of a particular market sector, let's say energy, banking, and other industries. What you have to do is to contribute the amount you are required, then wait for the transaction to be done and obtain revenue. At this juncture, you do not have to hustle on finding the right portfolios or choosing or reading the indicator to identify the area with the potential returns.

Think of the shareholders. What takes you to try to buy shares from that renowned company? You probably want to earn a lot of capital when the company makes profits. Anyway, do you actively engage in its affairs? Perhaps you do not even know its structure and directors leave alone the work done by that firm. What you will earn from those firms are the dividends that are shared according to your contribution. Therefore, at the warmth of your bed, you can anticipate the firms likely to make significant returns and place your odds in them.

Hey, do you know where the YouTubers make their money? Many

people do not recognize that it is a venture for the source of wealth. What you need is that lovely photograph and camera you have, and you make those funny jokes or videos you are talented. You will earn capital when people click on your ads or share; you still win. As long as you have uploaded your video on the internet, you will continue to earn cash as long as people view it. Therefore, utilize your talents and play them on YouTube to attain that extra income.

Still, in the online source of revenue, let consider an eBook. Yes, this type of online manual is very tedious to write because it involves a lot of literature. However, when it is certified for transmission over the internet, it will earn you more. It will even circulate to those who like it, and they continue sharing it. When they do that, you will realize how fast you will start earning that little penny. You will not even bother writing it again as the money continues coming.

The way the bloggers acquire that extra income is very significant. It only needs a blogger to have a renowned platform that is quality. That is where people like reading your articles and information. Therefore, traders will subscribe to your platform to advertise their business. If any of the firms do so, you will be surprised when you start earning sizeable income. In the meantime, you will not even be actively involved in your bog spot as the promos receive for you.

Some other sites of getting revenues can even be called semi-passive. Commensurate of those firms that sell their commodities online. You can say that they are actively involved as they control their market and the payment scheme. However, that is different from the hawking of products or selling using a shop. You have to photoshoot your products and exhibit them in the best way that is enticing to the customers. Then the consumers will also buy online and pay online.

You can invent an idea and sell it to a company in the contract that you earn a certain percentage of the profit they make. That is related to the selling of the royalties. These royalties include patents, copyrights, and trademarks. Therefore, the company that buys your idea has to pay you monthly. Consequently, you will be paid for something you are not working hard, but because you are the mother of that idea, they are generating their income. Licensing and franchising can also be attributed to such actions. That is where an established company lease it right to another growing one. You, like that established firm, you will be paid in the percentage you agreed in the franchising contract.

You need to save that extra penny of yours in the savings account in the bank. That can even be the fixed savings account that you are restricted from withdrawing the money. You can deposit money and state the period you want it to be kept safe. Consequently, you will be surprised at the rate your cash is accumulating. That is the interest rate that has caused such accumulation. In a simple sense, your money is gaining value by not actively investing in it. Therefore, that is a passive way of investing cash in the bank.

On the same idea, consider peer-to-peer lending. It uses the same principle as the saving s account. That is where you will lend the money to your friend with the promise that it will be refunded in some interest. The interest it has gained is the revenue you get when you are not involved in increasing its value. This type of lending is sometimes risky as there are many debt defaulters. Therefore, you have to identify the collateral to use if the loaned or debtor fails to pay the loan.

Steps in How You Can Train the Passive Income

The first thing that you ought to do is to have that business idea. That idea should be the locus to start on passive trading. If you are a landowner, that idea of owning a plot should first clock in your head. When you have that idea, research on it, know how it can be used to obtain finances without getting much involved. You should also engage other professional business-minded individuals to advise you accordingly.

The other thing to do is to save your cash to cater to the business you want. Remember that every opportunity requires capital to start. That is what is making young people not venture on many occasions because they still depend on their parents. You have to be aggressive in saving even the pocket money you are given in the school. For you to make others work for you must use a ransom of money. Moreover, when thinking about a passive venture, know that you are susceptible to paying higher taxes. Therefore, you must sacrifice the pleasure of today for the benefit of tomorrow.

In choosing the line of passive business, focus on income assets.

Remember that for the goods to attain this attribute, they must be easily liquefied and manageable. A complicated thing like scientific items cannot be passive as they need your knowledge to spearhead their selling. Think about investing in stocks, currencies, or other securities that make that higher capital. You have to oversee the cost of acquiring such assets as rentals and anticipate the marginal profit which it can gain.

When you are satisfied that the choice of business, then think of how it will earn you that extra income starts right away; moreover, sometimes starting a venture is occasionally tricky and needs a lot of cash. Do not be afraid of inputting your money into it because the business earnings will compensate you. If you have to write that eBook or make money for buying shares, be actively engaged in producing such items. Therefore, you will have that cost structure that you will use to evaluate how much passive you need.

In the knowledge of the passive capital you need, it will help you in multiple ways. One way is that you will have that tangible targets of the revenues you anticipate to make. Therefore, you will be motivated to work hard. It also offers you the bargaining power to loan some cash. Lastly, it will make you anticipate the profits you will amerce at the expense of the cost used.

When you have done so, then it is your time to put your ideas to work. Identify the channels of advertising your business. Employ those characters who you feel share your passion. Identify the suitable agents who will run your business for you, for example, the real estate business. Ensure that your assets and products are diversified. That is a strategy to ensure you compensate for the weakness of a trade with the strength of another.

Chapter 15: Why Options Trading is the World's Greatest Money-Making Machine?

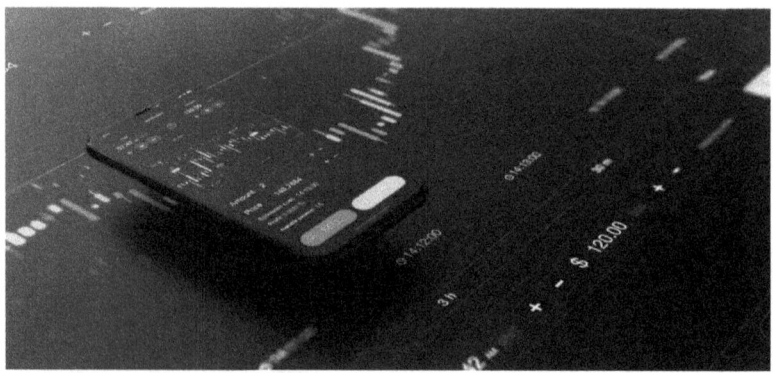

It's useful to know why we are trading options in the first place. The fact that they are cheap, is only one factor to consider. We are going to look at some of the specific benefits that come with trading options. Knowing what they are is going to help you make the right investment decisions.

Options Provide Leverage

When you buy an options contract, you control 100 shares of stock for the lifetime of that option. An option is a tool that allows you to control those shares of stock without paying the full price for them. For example, Apple may be trading at $200 a share. An options contract on

Apple might cost $125 for a particular strike price. Had I purchased the shares; the cost would be $200/share x 100 shares = $20,000. So, for 0.625% of the price of the shares, I can control the shares for the time until the options contract either expires or I sell it.

Options are Inexpensive

OK, this is kind of a restatement of the point above, but to buy shares you need a lot of money. Yes, you could buy one share of Apple, but if the price of Apple goes up to $1, what you've made is $1. To profit using shares of stock, say by swing trading, you need to own a lot of shares of stock. As we'll see in a minute price changes in the stock are magnified in the option. If Apple goes up to $1, the options trader is going to be a lot better off than the guy who only buys one share with his $200.

Options Prices Change in Big Ways

The price or value of an option is directly related to the share price of the stock. It's not a one-to-one relationship in most cases, however. We'll see what the exact value is, but for now, let's say a call option for Apple stock is going to move in such a way that for every dollar Apple gains and losses, the price of the option will move by $0.80. This is on a per-share basis – so for the option overall, a $1 move in the stock means an $80 move in the value of the option.

This cut both ways, so options trading is not for the faint of heart. It also requires discipline. If you are watching an option for a single day, you might see it go up and down by $50 in value if there is a lot of volatility. But the advantage is a small price increase in-stock can lead to big profits very quickly. Suppose that you bought that Apple option for $125. If the price per share of Apple goes up to $0.40, then the price of the option would rise to $157. Had it gone up to $1, the option would rise in price to $205.

Remember that goes both ways, so a decline in price by 40 cents would drop a $125 option to $93. Option prices can move fast throughout the day, so you have to be keeping a close eye on it so you don't get wiped out and take advantage of opportunities to sell for profits.

The amount that each option's price moves to the price of the underlying stock is something that varies depending on the individual option. We will discuss how to figure out the possible price changes later.

Options Have a Higher ROI

The return on investment for an option is much higher than for stocks. Let's say you had $5,000 to invest, and we used that to buy Apple shares at $200 a share. That would give us 25 shares. So, if the price went up by $2, that would give us a $50 profit, ignoring commissions. So, we'd have an ROI of:

ROI = $50/$5,000 x 100 = 1%

That isn't a bad share increase for a single day move, investors in stocks are looking for a return of maybe 8% per year.

We could buy 40 options contracts at $125 each. Using the previous example where a $1 move in the stock increases the per-share price of the option by $0.80 a $2 price increase would raise the price of the option from $125 to $285. The total profit per option contract is $160. Our net profit with $0 commissions on Robin Hood would be $6,400. The ROI in the case of the option is:

ROI = $6,400/$5,000 x 100 = 128%

There are even bigger opportunities than this, on certain days you'll see stocks make big moves, like after an earnings announcement. The share price could go up to $10 or $20 if earnings beat expectations. The opportunities for profits are enormous.

Options are Flexible

It's common to talk about call options because the concept is easier for beginners to understand, but put options give the options trader advantages a stock investor doesn't have. What if instead, the stock price of Apple dropped $2? In that case, the investor in the Apple stock would lose $50 instead. It's not a huge loss to be sure, but a loss is a loss.

But a clever options trader who saw the decline coming could have bought put options with their money. For the sake of simplicity, assuming that the price of the option was the same and it related to the stock price in the same way, the price of the put options would go up by

$6,400 when the price of Apple dropped $2.

And we'll see later that you can devise strategies that will earn profits no matter which way the stock price moves. These techniques go by the name of the straddle, strangle, and iron condor among others.

Options are Fast

Options have an expiration date. Some people will see this as a negative, but others will find it refreshing. Since options have an expiration date, they are not assets that you're going to hold onto very long (except for LEAPS). For those that like an asset with an expiration date, the result of this on a practical level is that with options you are going to get in and get out of your trades pretty quickly. You might periodically do day trades when a stock is experiencing large price movements. I typically do 2-3 a week (remember don't do 4 a week, unless you plan to deposit $25,000 and accept the day trader designation). In most cases, you'll hold the option for a couple of days and then sell it when the opportunity arises. If you are selling to open, then you'll be holding the position for anywhere from a week to a month or two. But there is no long-term investing.

Conclusion

Now it's time to step it up and enter the world of success in trading options. And you have to set up a bonafide trading objective to do so! More than just that. You need to come up with a specific monetary purpose.

Are you just investigating some fundamental knowledge of the trading of options? In options trading, are you new to getting started? If so, realize that there is a whole new world of opportunity for you out there. Start with a few hundred or a few thousand dollars, and you can make millions of dollars! And don't let any person ever tell you otherwise.

Remember that successful business people concentrate on what they want. They make goals and focus on the targets. Failures concentrate on the risks and focus on their fears and problems or potential future issues. What is your intended purpose if you are involved in the online trading of options? Yes, that is a very significant point. To get involved in online options trading, you need to have a particular purpose. About why? Because you can get quickly distracted and off course in options trading, confused and lose focus of any original concept she had that inspired you to join options trading.

I have found from my experience that it is crucial to have a trading objective, a financial trading goal. In trading online options, it is important because having an economic purpose will help you bring everything together and acquire the knowledge and tools you need to succeed to get you to that goal. So, in other words, if you set sail at sea without a particular destination, unless you have unlimited fuel. You're going to be in trouble. The same goes for trading online options. And in trading online options, if you don't have an overall trading goal, you could either not make much money or lose money.

Once you have a trading objective, all you need is to master the book's strategies, and you will fly high in the trading world of options.

CPSIA information can be obtained
at www.ICGtesting.com
Printed in the USA
BVHW080231020321
601389BV00003B/424